Rock Star Publishing
ISBN: 978-1-9995503-1-8

ALSO BY JULIE FAIRHURST
Agent Etiquette: 14 Things That You Didn't Learn In Real Estate School (The Keys To Your Success Series)

Workbook designed by Angelique Duffield
https://brightsparkwebsitedesign.com

BULK PURCHASES
For bulk purchases of this workbook, please contact the author directly at:
julie@rockstarstrategies.com

HOW TO USE THIS GUIDE

I've taken my 30 years of real estate experience and distilled it into a step by step guide that will help you build a successful career as a real estate agent.

This workbook is broken down into daily activities. Or you could sit down and work for an entire day and brainstorm your answers, then come back and add more details later.

When you are ready to take action, you could print out the guide and hand write your answers (use the back of the page if you need more space).

However it was made to so that you could download the workbook, open in Adobe Acrobat, and then type your answers directly inside the sections. The fillable space scrolls so you can keep typing if you have a long answer. Be sure to save often!

Or you could freeform your answers in a Word or Google doc.

Do whatever feels right for you.

But... just do it!

INTRODUCTION

Welcome! I'm so excited for you to get started. Whether you are a brand-new agent in the business or a seasoned professional, just needing a bit of a jump start, you'll find the next 30 days will get you going.

You need to take action to get your business to bring you in some income, but what kind of activity is necessary? The last thing you want to do is waste 30 days of your career confused over what the best plan of action for you to take.

I am so tired of seeing agents come into the business, only a year or two years later to drop out. It takes a lot of effort to get your real estate license… and expense! And when they drop out, their dreams are crushed, and many will leave with some form of debt. Real estate is a great income earner, but it is also expensive. Every month that you don't make a sale, your office bill will continue to rise.

I have been selling real estate for nearly 30 years, selling over 2000 homes as a full-time real estate agent. I have developed systems that work. Systems that if followed will give you longevity in your real estate career.

Most of the systems I teach are "boots on the ground" sales strategies. I'm putting the REAL back in real estate. Teaching real connections and real strategies that work.

I know if you follow these 30 strategies, and take the action required, you will have built a solid ground on which to grow your business.

I wish you all the success you desire.

Because everyone deserves to live their best life.

Julie

DAY 01

SETTING UP YOUR COMMUNICATION TOOLS

Of course, this sounds like common sense; you need to set up your devices for business. But not everyone gets it professionally!

PHONE
Make sure you have lots of room for voice mail, nothing worse than getting the message, "this person's mailbox is full." Or even worse, "this person has not initialized their voice mail system yet."

Be friendly. Mention your full name and the company where you have your license. Tell them you are sorry you missed their call, but it is important to you, and if they leave a message, you'll get right back to them.

Your voice mail may be the first time your potential client hears your voice, speak clearly and sound friendly.

EMAIL
What is your email address? Don't use something from 10 years ago that doesn't even relate to real estate! It needs to be professional.

Remember, not just the general public will be emailing you, but so will lawyers, notaries, mortgage brokers, other agents. Use a professional email address.

And don't forget to have a courteous salutation when you reply. Be friendly. Be professional.

BUSINESS CARDS
Be professional, put your photo on it with your direct contact information. Depending on the rules for your area and real estate board, make sure you are complying.

With regards to business cards, I'd have maybe 100 to start with because once you get out there, handing them out and seeing what others are doing, you may want to adjust them. Save money by ordering a small amount to start.

Take a few minutes right now while you are focusing on your communication tools. Make a note of what you want your voicemail and email message to be when others hear it. As well, what is vital for you to have on your business cards.

Then record your voicemail message. Oh, but don't sound like you're reading it! Have some excitement and happiness in your voice.

DAY 02

BRANDING - WHO ARE YOU AS A REAL ESTATE AGENT?

Have you thought about what your message is going to be to the world? You will be putting out a message, and it's up to you what you'll say. It's essential to brainstorm what you want your message to be.

What are personality traits you have that will attract a buyer or seller? Did you grow up in the area, or if not, how long have you lived here.

Did you come from another industry? For example, I know nurses and police officers who retire then use their old career to market to those who are still in that industry.

Do you speak a different language? Do you read or write a different language? What is unique about you that you can highlight?

YOUR PHOTO

I can't emphasize this enough, get professional photos. A real professional. Don't run up to where you can get a passport photo and try to use that. You need to have a professional take your picture. Remember this is a marketing tool for you; this is what you will put out there. Be professional.

And no kids, dogs, cats, fish, cars, boats... you get the drift. If you want to add lifestyle photos of you later for your social media, you can, and lifestyle photos are great for social media.

But when it comes to business cards and websites, make sure it is very professional.

COLORS

What colors will you use in your branding? It's imperative as the colors you choose may not look professional. Do some research on colors before you decide which one to use. Make sure it's a color that works with your photo and your message.

WORDING

Here is where you will put it all together. Your expert statement, your message, slogan if you are going to use one, your photo... this is where it all should flow together.

Also, consider writing an elevator speech/statement. You can research what this is if you have not heard of it before.

You want to have a quick, short to the point statement to tell someone when they ask what you do. If you can write this ahead of time, you will not stress out when the question gets asked, "What is it that you do?"

Write down your favorite color, your favorite fonts, any ideas that you think would be great for your branding or what makes you unique. Do it now, and then you can refer back when you are ready to get started.

DAY 03

WITH WHOM DO YOU WANT TO WORK?

Now, this may sound confusing if you are a new agent in the business, with not a lot of experience. Or if you've been around the block, you most likely understand the different buyer and seller types, and you will already know who you love to work with and who you don't.

Either way, you will need to decide who you want to focus on to start building your business.

Marketing can encompass all the types of buyers and sellers, but if you want to be an expert (and I strongly suggest you do), then you will need to direct your marketing to that group of potential clients.

It doesn't mean you will not work with other types, because you will! But specializing and becoming an expert in one client type will kick start your career.

FIRST TIME HOMEBUYERS

This buyer will need a lot of hand-holding through the buying process. It is an exciting time for them, and they may be all over the map when it comes to searching for their first home.

You'll find you may need to take control so, you can guide them in the right direction. First-time buyers can be a lot of work, but a lot of fun as well.

SENIORS

I love working with this group. Yes, they can be grumpy, but they are also delightful. This group is very loyal and if they trust you, will work with you.

You may find though that it is a long process for nurturing them. Seniors tend to stay where they are until they must move. However, if you have been contacting them, over the years, they will remember you and call you when the time comes to sell.

One drawback with Seniors is that when they sell, they usually do not buy again. Some, do, but many will move onto a retirement home.

BOOMERS

This group is usually downsizing from their home. Kids are gone, yard work too much, they want fewer headaches and crave freedom. They usually will interview more than one agent and choose the agent they feel will be a good fit for them.

The great thing is that they will also buy, as they usually do not leave the market. Therefore, if working with Boomers, you be looking at two transactions.

MOVE UP BUYERS

Almost any age group can be a move up buyer. They are moving out of their first home and into something, usually a little more expensive and generally larger. Maybe looking for their "forever home."

This buyer is most likely a first-time home seller. They will have a basic idea of what is involved in selling their home.

This type of client will be doing two transactions. They will stay in the market.

INVESTORS

Working with this type of client can be great. They are usually known to be knowledgeable with the process of buying and selling. They are also quick to make their decision as buying or selling real estate for them is not an emotional process.

Due to no emotion in the process, they are focused on dollars and cents. If it doesn't make sense financially, it's not happening.

NEW HOME SALES

You may want to sell brand new developments. Either as an agent representing the buyer or directly for the developer. It can be a fantastic way to get experience in the business and connect with lots of potential clients, if lucky enough to find a developer willing to work with you.

They usually are looking for some experience in the agents they hire. You don't need to be a seasoned agent, but you do need to know what you are doing.

No matter who you decide to work with, remember that you want to be able to be the specialist or expert in the field.

What is it about each of these groups that appeals to you? And what is it that you dislike? Once you have decided which group to focus your attention on, what is it about you that will be a benefit to them?

DAY 04

FARMING AND UNDERSTANDING YOUR MARKET

Now that you know who you want to work with let's get your farming in place.

Don't be a jack of all trades. You can work with anyone and sell anything, but when it comes to farming, you want to be the expert.

You can farm a neighborhood, building, area or group of people. We already covered who you want to work with, go back over that section if you are still unsure.

Once you know, then immerse yourself in your farm. If you decide later you want to work with a different group or property type, no biggie, you can do that. Just don't get super hung up on the process.

Set yourself up on auto notification for the area. Set up an auto-notification for any real estate activity that happens, so you are on top of it and know right away what is going on.

Get out to open houses, see everything that is on the market.

Join online community groups, participate, show you are there. Gently, don't jump in and start telling them all about you and get them to work with you; it should be soft and gentle.

The key to success with farming is consistency and being in it for the long haul. If you can do this, the rewards are amazing.

In one building I have sold 74 (yes) resale homes, another building 27, yet another 18. There are so many buildings where I have an average of 10 -12 sales and continue to get more business in those buildings.

There is an art to it, way too much to go into detail here. If you want more detail on farming, then connect with me, and we can go from there!

What are you going to do to get started in your farm area? Write down all your ideas of how to take over your farm area and be the local expert that buyers and sellers will call when they are ready to do business?

DAY 05

YOUR ONLINE PRESENCE

You will need a website, but until you get that under your belt, you can start with the social media sites. These are generally free to use, so it's a great resource to get started with right away.

Remember, in anything you do with regards to marketing, use your brand. You want to be recognized by your name, photo, and branding. That is key to being known. It's super important.

You can get on Facebook, Instagram, Zoho Social, Friends and Me, Yelp, Pinterest, Followerwonk, Linkedin, and any others that you may want to use.

Snoop around, what are others doing on social media? Don't full out copy them but get some ideas of what others are doing to be successful with their social media.

You will need to have a business page, aside from a personal page. Be sure you research the rules for each social media site you plan on using. Follow the rules. You do not want to have thousands of followers and then have your page shut down because you were using your personal page when it should have been a business page.

Word of caution! What is on social media with regards to you? Google yourself and check it out. If there is anything that could hurt your business, do your best to get rid of it.

You can hire a professional to set up your social media and posts if that is helpful. Remember, as in everything you do, be professional.

Jot down a few notes now with regards to where you want to start your business page. What types of posts will you do? What will you focus on?

DAY 06

KNOW YOUR PRODUCT

Do you know your product? Luckily for you, now that you're an agent you have access to plenty of listings to view and get information at your fingertips.

Go to open houses. Take a family member or friend along with you as your client. Practice the process of visiting open houses. If you practice, you'll feel good and at ease when you visit with your buyer.

Visit brand new developments and gather brochures and any other information you can get your hands on. Save these brochures and one day, when you have a listing appointment there, you will slide their floor plan in the presentation and dazzle them that you are so on it.

Visit anything on lockbox especially if it is vacant. When a property is vacant, and the listing agent has a lock box on it, these are great to view as you are not putting the seller or agent out with your viewing. It can be a great way to get out there and see what sellers are selling and what they are asking in price.

The only way to know your product, and to be knowledgeable in the area you are working, is to get out there and view as much as possible. Why not set a day and time that you will commit to each week to get out into the real estate world and get to learn about your product?

What are some of the ways you will get to know your product?

DAY 07

YOUR LISTING PRESENTATION MATERIAL

Congratulations! You have an appointment. Or maybe not yet. But are you ready when you do get that important call? Then what? What are you planning on walking in with to your appointment? I have won many times over three and four other agents just because of my presentation I take with me.

What will you use? Don't just walk in with a stack of unorganized papers, shuffling through while you're sitting with the sellers. Trust me, they will notice. And what if you are up against a few other agents, as we all know, they usually will interview a few agents. What will set you apart from the others?

Your presentation will!

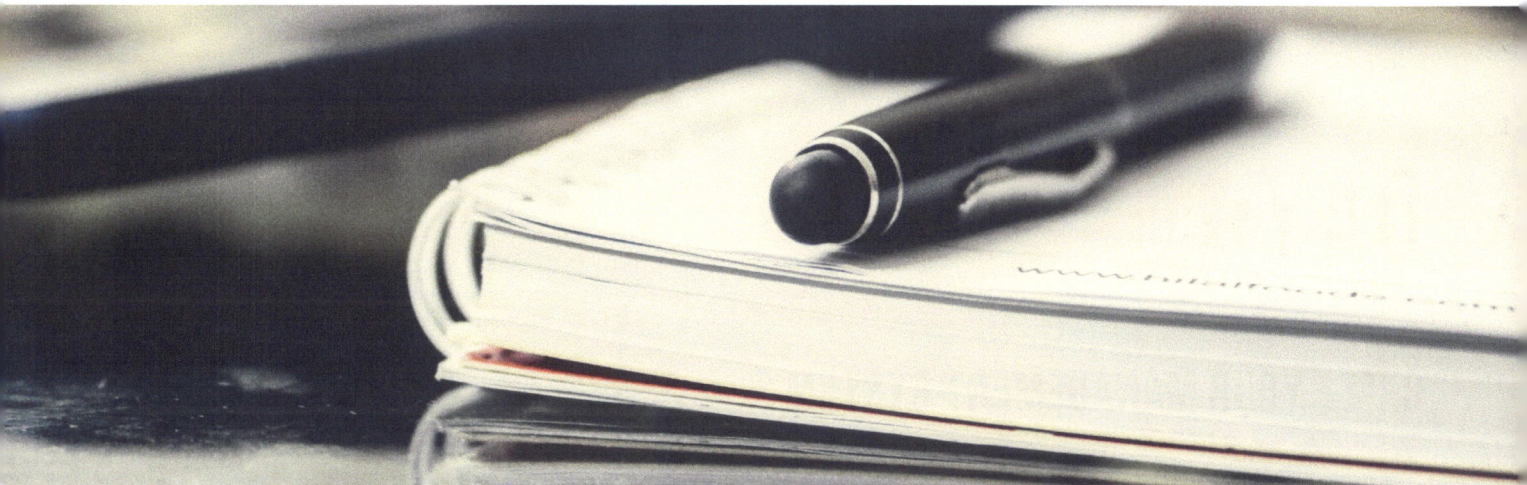

You may want to have it designed with your branding, and create a professional presentation that you can take with you when you go.

There is a list of items, depending on the type of property the seller owns, that you will want to include. For our purposes here, be sure you at least have the following....

1) Cover sheet
2) Your information
3) Some marketing information
4) Information about the seller's property
5) Comparable properties

Paper or Paperless? I believe paper, all the way. Not everyone appreciates an online presentation. Should the seller need time to decide who to list their home with, they will have your information at their fingertips to peruse at their leisure.

Many times, after leaving my presentation for the seller, I get the call that I won the listing!

With my coaching clients, I have a program that is a step-by-step strategy of what you should include. If you would like more details, contact me.

Make a list of the items you will need for your listing presentation.

DAY 08

CRM - YOUR MANAGEMENT SYSTEM

A CRM (customer relationship management) program is going to be extremely important for the success of your business.

If you are new to CRM, it is a strategy for managing your relationship with your clients. As well as nurturing future clients. CRM will help you stay connected.

There are several you can use in your business. You will need to find the one that works for you.

Some have prepared letters, cards, and other marketing pieces. You can set up an email campaign. There are some that now includes "text" message automation. Technology has come a long way.

A few of the CRM that I see my students use and a few that I use are listed below. You can have a look and see what works. Of course, there are many others, find what works for you. The key here though is to have one and use it.

Hubspot	Zoho
Ixact	Pipedrive
Claritysoft CRM	Gold-Vision CRM
Maximizer CRM	Insightly
Salesmate	Monday.com
Freshsales	Act by Swiftpage

What categories will be vital for you to have in your CRM? Birthdays. Anniversary Dates. Move in Dates. Where they work? Take time now to develop a list of information that you will be using to gather data on your prospective clients.

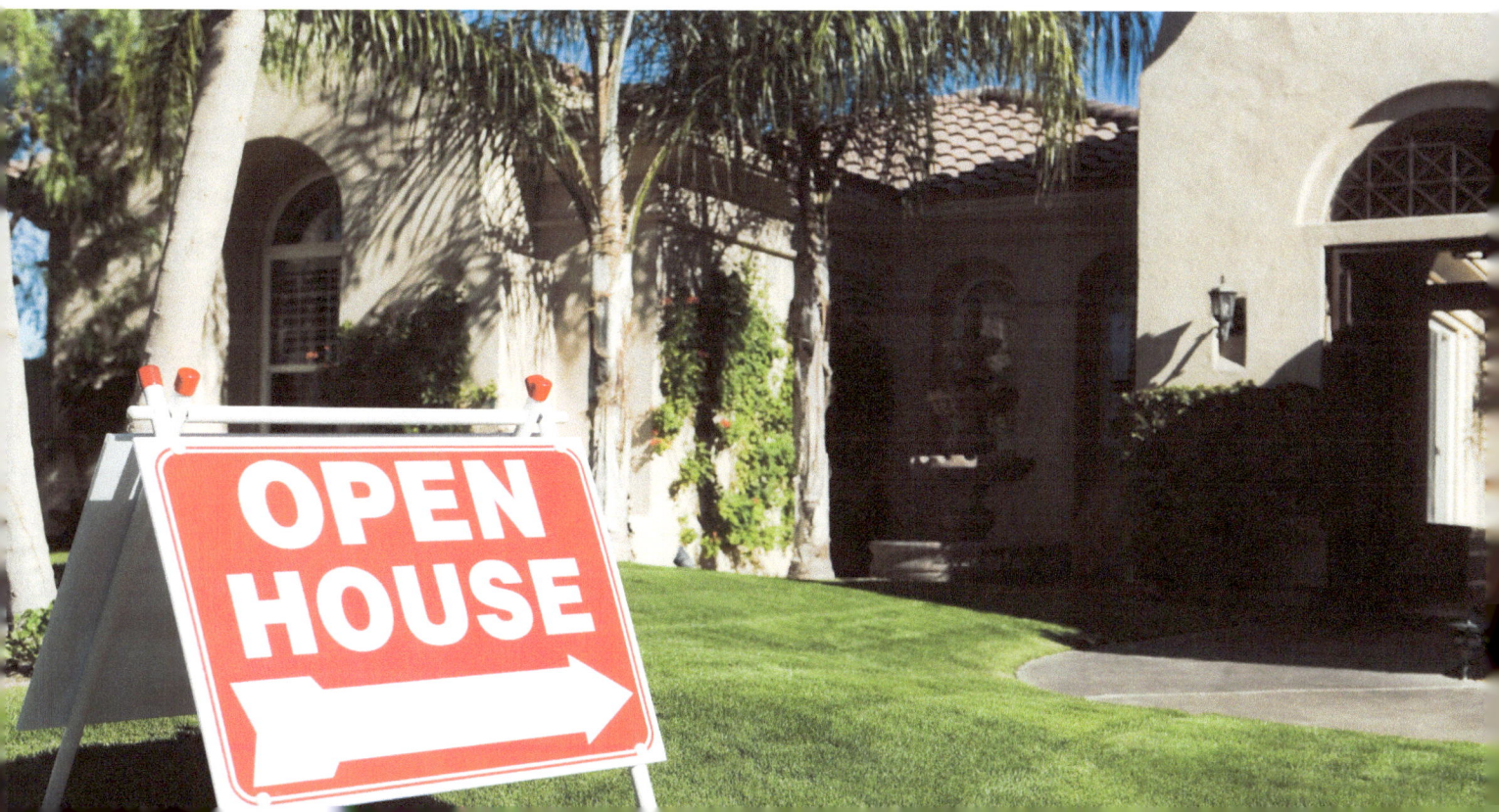

DAY 09

DO OPEN HOUSES

Find someone in your office that has plenty of listings that they would love to have you hold an open house.

The goal, of course, is to hope that the golden prospect walks into your open house, falls in love with the home and writes an offer, with you. Even if that golden prospect doesn't walk through the door, consider this a great learning experience in dealing with the general public and answering questions.

Open houses can also be a valuable tool for picking up buyers who are not working with other agents. Also, this is your chance to chat with the neighbors, who most likely will pop in for a look.

Most of the people walking into an open house are there because they are thinking of buying. They very well could be there because they are checking out the competition as they are getting their home ready for sale. What a fantastic opportunity for you to shine and hopefully get a chance to present yourself to them when they are prepared to hire an agent.

As a new agent or an agent who is trying to kick start your business, open houses can and have shown to be, a valuable tool and a key to your success.

What tools will you take to your open house? Will you take feature sheets to highlight the property and you? Also, think of your safety. An open house is open to anyone who wants to come in. How will you protect yourself?

DAY 10

OFFICE LISTINGS

What is the rule in your area? In my area, the brokerage "owns" the listings. So, we advertise each others' listings, where ever we like!

It's a brilliant idea! And why would anyone care, meaning the listing agent? Please, sell my listing! The brokerage owns the listings, so the seller's permission to have everyone in the office advertise it is not required. (Check for the rules in your area, always!)

The goal is undoubtedly to attract a buyer to buy the home, but even if you can't sell them the property, you hopefully will pick them up, as buyers. Business is business, no matter if it is a buyer or a seller.

If a listing agent does not want to participate, then that's okay, find the ones that do. I would never say no to another agent from my office wanting to advertise my listing. Hey, the goal is to get it sold right?

Just be sure you know the rules for your area and brokerage.

Who could you approach in your office to advertise their listings? What are the rules for your office? Once you get permission, where will you promote them?

DAY 11

ASK FOR LEADS

From EVERYONE!

Yes, everyone, you can think of in your world. Who might that person know, who may be thinking of selling or buying real estate? You will be surprised how many people will want to help you with your success. Most of us love to help, but you have to ask, or we don't know.

How do you ask? In person, you can call, or you can send out a letter, card or flyer letting everyone you know, know that you are ready for business.

If people don't know you are an agent ready to work, they will not think of you. Real estate is a strange business where we need to keep in front of everyone and continually remind them that we are ready and that we appreciate referrals!

Make a list of everyone you can think of who you can ask for a buyer or seller lead.

DAY 12

CONTRACTS, TOOLS OF THE TRADE.

You are out there, your marketing is up and running, and you're waiting for that prospective client to contact you to do business. Are you ready and comfortable with filling out the paperwork?

If there is ever a tip for great success, it would be to know your paperwork, inside, outside and upside down. If you can't fill out a listing agreement, buyers agency agreement or a purchase agreement and you can't explain them to your client, well that's not good at all.

Read the paperwork over and over again. You should highlight areas where you need clarity. Ask your manager. Or even ask other agents. It is a must to understand those forms. Those forms are going to make you money. Using those forms is the ONLY way you will make money.

Know your paperwork, word for word and be sure you are comfortable explaining them to your clients. It's one of the best things you can do for your success.

Make a list of the paperwork you will need to work with a buyer and what you will need to work with a seller.

DAY 13

SIGN UP FOR CLASSES

You've been working for a bit now. Are you feeling more comfortable about all this real estate stuff?

Next step is to sign up for some courses! Now you're probably thinking, yeah right, it's the last thing I want to do. And hey, I get it.

But there is so much that you don't know. Trust me, so many little things.

The interesting thing about real estate is that there are a million things to know. After nearly 30 years, and over 2000 sales, I'm still surprised by some situations.

Think about it. You are dealing with different types of properties, different buyers and seller personalities, in different locations. There will always be something new you will learn.

As well, keep on top of new regulations that are forever changing. You will need to stay on top of what is going on. Our industry will demand it of you. And if you want to do things right, keeping you out of hot water (and your client), you will need to be learning continually.

What interests you right now that you could learn more about? What do you feel you could be lacking in and a bit of learning would help?

DAY 14

MODEL SUCCESSFUL AGENTS

Fourteen days in, you must have met some fantastic real estate agents. Is there anyone you look up too? If so, what are the qualities that you admire?

There is nothing wrong with modeling a successful agent. We learn from others.

Watch the things successful agents do and do those things? Watch the way successful agents conduct themselves and do that. Listen to how successful agents speak and use their language.

And if you're feeling brave enough (don't be scared) ask those successful agents for a little bit of advice. They will be happy to share their success with you.

Make a list of questions you may like to ask an agent that you admire. And make a list of who you will ask.

DAY 15

RELAX

You have been at this for fifteen days now. If you are like most agents, I suspect you have worked every one of those days.

Do something kind for yourself. Spend some time with your friends and family.

Forward your phone to the office and only return calls that will make you money. Be very picky about what you do today.

You need to schedule a time for you. Now, I know just how hard this can be, super hard. Real estate is a "turn on a dime" type of business. You have worked all day, now you are sitting down for dinner, and your email or phone wants your attention. Maybe it's an offer (yay you'll make some money), and you must deal with it.

Be sure to take your downtime when you can. You never know when you'll get another chance.

Make a list of what you love to do and who you want to share your time? It's time to take time for you.

DAY 16

TIME MANAGEMENT

It's so easy to lose track of time, especially in the real estate industry. It's a very social business and there is always something fun just around the corner. Be careful not to get too caught up in the office lunches that can drag on for hours. Or the office time wasters who want to stop at your door while you are trying to get some work done, who are standing there demanding your attention, talking about nothing important.

Get yourself on a schedule. Get up at a specific time of day. Go to the office early. I love getting to the office before anyone else. I'm always more productive.

Depending on your day, if you have no evening appointments then go home and spend some downtime. You may find you are out most evenings working your behind off. So, if you have downtime, use it.

Do you find you are someone who runs late regularly? If so, you will have trouble in this industry. Real estate is a people-based business, and most likely, you will have people waiting for you. Buyers to view properties, other agents waiting for you, prospective clients booking appointments to interview you to sell their home, even the weekly sales meeting.

If you have an issue with time management, now is the time to get over it. Figure out why you are late and fix it. You are going to have trouble if you don't and it is going to hit you in your bank account.

Make being on time a top priority, and it will pay off in the long run, big time.

DAY 17

WORKING A PARTNERSHIP

Do you think you need a real estate partner? Or has someone approached you to see if you want to team up with them?

Teams can be great! You can share income and cover for one another during illness or holidays. You will also have someone to mastermind with about growing the business.   There is a real benefit in being partners with another agent.

Be careful though. There are downsides as well. Is this person going to work as hard as you? Do you have the same work ethic? Nothing worse than you having to take up the slack for someone who is quite happy to dump the workload on you.

Another issue to concern yourself with is as a partnership, if both your names are on all contracts and listing agreements, this means you will be held responsible for what your team members does or says. You will each take responsibility for each other's actions.

Lastly, how does this person conduct themselves around the clients or the public in general? Are they professional, polite, courteous and conscientious? You don't want to lose clients or potential clients because you are partners with someone who can't control their emotions or verbiage.

As partners, if your partner lacks professionalism, the public and other agents will think you do too. After all, you're partners, right?

What benefits could a partnership have? How could a partnership help you?

DAY 18

NURTURE YOUR LEADS

I could write a book here for you. There are so many beautiful ways to nurture your leads. Let me give you a few of my favorites to get you going.

You can send handwritten notes or cards. These are wonderful, and everyone loves to get something in the mail. Not email. Snail mail. Why would you send them a handwritten card? Because 99% of the other agents won't!

You went on a listing appointment? Send a thank you note. You have a great conversation with someone? If you can get their address, send a little note.

If you don't know their address, then an email or short text message works. The key here is to send something.

Updates on real estate are excellent for nurturing prospective clients, and they love it. I'm not a fan of the recipes or random things. I like to stay real estate related. After all, you are in real estate, not the food industry, be sure your information is always real estate related.

You can drop by for a quick visit. Maybe you have a small, inexpensive gift you can deliver.

What is the season? You could deliver a pumpkin or a few little candy hearts or a poinsettia. We have so many holidays you could drop by once a month with a small gift.

If there is a change in the real estate industry, maybe a fantastic interest rate deal or something you think would benefit them, tell them.

Nurturing the relationship is easy. You just have to do it. Get a calendar or a whiteboard and jot down all the holidays. Then you can decide which one and what you'll drop off or mail to your client or potential client.

What's happening in the community? Is there a children's festival at the local park or a senior's breakfast or a dog show? Keep in the loop and share these events with others, they will appreciate it.

The key is to keep in touch. As much as possible without being overwhelming. The goal is when the prospect is ready to do business your name and face is top of mind.

Write out some ways you would like to nurture your clients and prospective clients. Don't over think it.

DAY 19

TIME TO BLOG

Yes, you must blog! You don't have to write long-winded blogs. Your blogs can be short and sweet, to the point.

Not sure what your blog subject should be? First remember that you sleep, breath and eat real estate. The general public does not. You already know so much more than they do. One thing I like about blogging is the research that I do to find subjects to write about. Researching real estate subjects gives me even more knowledge for my business.

The internet is a fantastic source of information, and no matter what it is that you want to know, you'll be able to find some information.

You may want to do video blogs. You could do short 90 second videos, quickly highlighting your topic. You could do podcasts.

There are so many ways to blog. The key is to do it. You are the real estate expert, and they want to hear from you.

When thinking of real estate, what subjects would you like to blog about? What do you think others will want to hear from you?

DAY 20

SALES SCRIPTS

I'm not a fan of memorizing word for word sales scripts. If you sound canned, the prospective client will hear it and right away you will lose credibility.

What I suggest is to write out how you will deal with this objection or question. Once you have thought it through put it on paper and read it over to yourself, do this several times. Not to memorize it, but to become comfortable with it.

When you are speaking with someone, no matter if in person or on the phone, you want to sound genuine and not scripted, practice what you will say, so it becomes natural to you. You can find another agent to practice with or a family member.

The more you practice, the easier it will be for you.

Take a few minutes and write out answers to questions your prospective client may ask? What types of objections will you need to overcome? Now is an excellent time to write out your script.

DAY 21

TIME WASTERS

How many viewings with a buyer of a property are too many? How many offers on a property that are rejected by the seller (assuming they are reasonable offers) are too many?

Be careful of the time wasters out there. It's tough to let go of someone with whom you have put in many hours of your time and expense. However, sometimes we need to cut our losses.

I never considered it a waste of my time, even if it didn't result in a paycheque in the end. Consider it learning, product knowledge and gaining experience.

In the end, if you dislike someone and know they are a time waster, it can feel excellent to "fire" them and move on.

Don't get yourself bogged down with someone who has no intention of buying or selling real estate. Sometimes, it takes a while to realize what is happening, but when you do, it feels good to cut them loose.

What are some ways you can recognize people who are just a waste of your time and what will you do to rid yourself of them... in a professional manner?

DAY 22

WORKING FROM HOME OR OFFICE

I am a total believer in working from the office, not at home daily. When you get up and get dressed for business, heading into the office for a day's work, it can feel pretty good.

There are others there with similar goals, in a fast-paced working environment. This type of work environment can be motivating and helpful to keep you moving forward.

When you work from home, daily, it can be isolating. You could go days without physically seeing anyone other than your immediate family. Working from home can cause you to lose motivation and become out of touch with others.

Some of us think how wonderful it would be to sit in our jammies all day long while working from home.

Maybe in the short term, but to have long term success you need to get into the world of the living.

What do you think the benefits are for you working at the office verses from home? Which will you choose?

DAY 23

GOAL SETTING

You're still here, and it's day 23! Congratulations keep up the excellent work.

Have you ever set goals? Do you believe in goal setting?

There have been studies conducted around the success of those who set goals. Some studies have shown a fantastic difference in people's lives who set defined goals over those who have no goals at all.

The key to goal setting, the one step that some people find difficult to do is to put your goals on paper. It is not enough to have goals, but the goals should be written down, in detail. A benefit to writing them down is now you can go back and review them and read them over daily.

Doing this will accelerate the procession of achieving the goals you have set. Why not take a few minutes now and write out your goals? Even just 5 or 10 goals, if you are struggling with not knowing what your goals are.

Magic will happen when you take the time to write out your goals.

Let's get you started on goal setting. Write out at least ten goals you would like to achieve. They can be immediate goals or more short-term goals. The key is to get them written down.

DAY 24

HOW TO STAND OUT

Don't get bogged down with how to stand out, it's not that difficult.

The main thing is you want the public to see your name. Your name, the one that you use for your real estate business. It is imperative that you use your name and that you are consistent.

How do you stand out? Everywhere and anywhere you can.

Social media is not too hard and is inexpensive because unless you are paying for the post, it is usually free.

On social media, make sure you like other people's posts. Make neutral comments here and there. Caution! Never anything negative or unpopular.

Even if you don't agree with whatever it may be. Think before you hit that enter button. Stay away from controversial subjects; it will only lead to less business, stay as neutral as possible.

Drop your business card where ever you can. Pin it on bulletin boards if it's allowed.

Renting a bus bench or several is a great way to get noticed. And if you can get it in your farm area, that would be excellent exposure for you.

Can you put just listed listing sheets anywhere in public? Some banks will partner with you or mortgage brokers to allow you to post in some of their locations.

Send out letters. Send out flyers. Try a newspaper ad. Get on Craig's list, and any other internet site you think would work.

The more the public sees your name, (and your face too) the more they will remember you, and when it comes time to buy or sell real estate, you will be top of their mind.

Write down all the ways you will stand out.

DAY 25

TIME TO MASTERMIND

Join a group of networking people. Masterminding is a fantastic thing to do. Be with like-minded individuals that are moving forward with their businesses and towards success.

You don't need to mastermind with other real estate agents. It can be any business group.

If you can't find a group to join, why not start your own? It will be easy to find 4 or 5 people that would like to meet regularly to share ideas and support one another.

There are mastermind groups on social media as well. Search them out and ask to join.

Masterminding will keep you motivated and get your creative juices flowing because you will also be helping others. When you help others, you are also helping yourself.

What subject would you like to use for a mastermind group? List different topics you would like to learn more about. What types of groups or people do you want to mastermind with?

DAY 26

THE LISTING APPOINTMENT

You have your listing appointment! This is a super exciting time.

Be prepared. Drive by the property if not familiar with the area. This is very important. Many times, I have headed to my listing appointment, only to turn onto their street and find a for sale sign or even worse, one with a sold sticker on it which did not come up in my search.

Get your presentation together. Add all the necessary documents you think the seller will need to help them see why you are valuing their home as you are.

Dress the part. If you are going on a listing appointment for a valuable property, be sure to look polished. If it is a lower end home, look presentable and professional. But don't head in with your thousand-dollar suit on. People like to work with people who are similar to them. Give it some thought before you head over to meet them.

I have a program, teaching agents what to do from the moment you get the listing appointment, to walking out the door with the signed listing paperwork. If you are interested in learning more, **feel free to reach out to me.**

For here though, the most important thing I can emphasize is to ASK FOR THE BUSINESS. Make sure you ask. Many times, I didn't think they were moving forward right then and there, but when I asked, they said okay let's do it.

It's easy, when you are finished your listing presentation, ask if they are ready to move forward.

Practice what you'll say so you are comfortable. Don't be shy. The owner wants you to ask. They are expecting it.

If you can't ask them for their business, why would they think you could close a buyer on their home.

Make a list here of what you'll need to prepare for when going on listing appointments.

DAY 27

WHAT KIND OF PROSPECTOR ARE YOU?

I don't know what kind you are, but I can tell you that you had better be consistent and be prospecting every single day. Don't fall into the busy pitfall and put prospecting last on your list.

I see so many agents, get a little bit of business, throw themselves into it 100%, then once they get that pay cheque, they realize no buyers or sellers are sitting at their doorstep.

So, the prospecting cycle continues. There is stress as the office bill rises, the visa bill hits its limit, and no deals are waiting to close at the office.

Take time every single day to prospect. Daily prospecting is key to your success.

Write out a list of ways that you will prospect for new business.

DAY 28

MAKE IT EASY TO DO BUSINESS WITH YOU.

Get off your high horse. Put your ego aside and let's do some business together. Help me help you sell your listing or let me help you sell your buyer my listing.

There are some agents out there that are not cooperative when it comes to working together. Egos get in the way, and well, it makes it painful to work together. And yes, we are working together, for a common goal.

My buyer wants to buy, and your seller wants to sell. We need to do what we can to make this happen for our clients.

Be cooperative. Be easy to get along with. Answer your phone, return that email, get those documents that are required. Help me if I am new and making mistakes.

Your sellers and buyers will see how you are working for them. Other agents will gain respect for you.

How can you make it easier for prospective clients and other agents do business with you?

DAY 29

HOW WILL YOU STAY MOTIVATED

Of course, you are motivated now, and you have been working daily kick-starting your sales career. But what happens on day 35 or day 75 moving forward?

Develop a plan for keeping you motivated daily.

What do you do in the morning? What do you do in the middle of the day? What do you do in the evening?

The internet is full of motivation videos, find some that resonate with you and watch them daily. Many people put their motivation videos on for you for free. Make use of this fantastic free resource.

Get some motivational CD's and listen in your car while your driving to appointments. Or find a radio station that has motivational subjects for you to hear. In real estate, you'll find your spending a lot of time in your car, make good use of your time.

Find some motivational books that you like and read a chapter here and there throughout the day.

The key to your success is getting a routine that works for you. Real estate can be a tough business, and at times it can be hard to stay motivated.

Do everything you can to keep your mindset strong and positive.

What are some ways that you can keep motivated?

DAY 30

YOU MADE IT!

Congratulations on your commitment to your success. You made it to day thirty.

Now, where do you go from here? You have a long career ahead of you, and this was just 30 days! Don't stop now. Do some business planning and some long and short term goal setting. Keep up the excellent work by developing a plan for your continued success.

It has been said; if you don't have a plan, then you are planning to fail. You don't think that is where you will end up, but if you don't have a daily plan for your business success, then you are not focused. If you are not focused, you will find you will be pulled this way and that, allowing distractions to take over your focus.

I can't express how vital writing your goals down is and reviewing them daily.

Do it now! Before you get distracted with other things. You'll be doing an excellent service to yourself.

What are your dreams and wishes for your life? Where do you want to be in one year, in five years or ten years?

WHAT'S NEXT?

I want to take the time to thank you for spending your time completing the 30 Days to Real Estate Action.

I sincerely hope it has helped you with your real estate business.

I invite you to book a free strategy call with me to discuss your business and how you can take it to the next level.

If you'd like to speak with me you can schedule a timeslot in my calendar on my website:

RockstarStrategies.com

I wish you all the success you desire.

Julie